Strange

Vigil

Strange Vigil

Scott Frey

BLACK LAWRENCE PRESS

For those laboring long watches over ailing beloveds.
And for Charlotte.

Black Lawrence Press

www.blacklawrence.com

Executive Editor: Diane Goettel

Chapbook Editor: Lisa Fay Coutley

Cover & Book Design: Zoe Norvell

Photograph of *Meditation Boats* (art by Susan Clinard) by Scott Frey

Published 2025 by Black Lawrence Press.

Printed in the United States.

TABLE OF CONTENTS

Plot Spoiler — 1

Roast Beef — 2

Passing the Bucket — 3

Making the Call After My Daughter's MRI — 4

New Mercies — 5

As Lawrence Timmons Tackles Derek Mason,
I Think of Home — 9

Night Nurses — 12

She Kept a Strange Vigil in the Hall That Night — 14

In the Circle — 16

In Praise of Dependence — 17

Through the Attic Window — 18

Charlotte's Blankets — 32

G-tube Ode — 34

Through the Concourse Din — 36

Acknowledgments — 43

About the author — 46

"You'll hear her voice sing-song around the ward
lifting a wing at the shore of your darkness."

LEANNE O'SULLIVAN, "Leaving Early"

"Then on the earth partially reclining sat by your side
leaning my chin in my hands,
    Passing sweet hours, immortal and mystic hours with
you dearest comrade—"

WALT WHITMAN, "Vigil Strange I Kept on the Field one Night"

Plot Spoiler

My wife's screams behind the bedroom door thicken like blood in a pot. Spots fill my vision like bile. Our five-month-old doesn't sleep more than half an hour, night or day. We've gone months like this. Sometimes she cries; sometimes she screams. Sometimes she sits wide-eyed in my arms, which is why I stay up all night with her and watch horror movies. Plot spoiler: she's having small seizures though we don't know it. Friends recommend the one where the mother moves into a haunted orphanage, the one where the girl is a witch who murders her family, the one where the girl with my daughter's name gets decapitated. The cinematography's brilliant when spirits reanimate her body. That's another plot spoiler. I can't stop writing them. The psychopath is already in the house, hiding in the basement. The twisted brother carves the hero into a hideous sculpture. It reanimates something in me that died when they told us of her mangled brain. The two of us are bonding over the young woman drenched in her friend's blood, pausing at the cornfield's edge. Framed against a pale farmhouse, tortured screams echoing in the night, she takes a deep breath. The chainsaw squeals.

Roast Beef

Of all the sandwiches we've shared from Nick's Famous Roast Beef, none tastes better than this. My teeth tear thin strips of red flesh. Grease streaks my fingers. Some dishes taste better lukewarm, hauled like a relic from a long line's wait to a distant dining room. This one's been delivered by my brother-in-law who drove here from the next state with my wife's entourage for her first labor and delivery. They roll deep. It's *a lahhge three-way* in North Shore parlance—cheese, mayo, and sweet jolt of sauce tasting how I picture our daughter kicking her way from the womb. He pretends to snap a photo with the blue-and-white bumper sticker logo for the restaurant wall. I wolf down the tender meat, drops of sauce dotting my shirt while her mom takes a shift at her side. Before I bolt back to her sweating twenty hours into that first mighty labor, I want to grab that younger self, pause him there on the gray carpet, his in-laws stuffed around him in the dim light of the birth center waiting room, hands halted mid-pat to his back. Dreams for wife and daughter mingling with the faint tang of antiseptic and a whiff of aftershave, the path still full of forks. Before the seizures and ambulance and brain injury, let this last meal linger: sauce burning the tongue, a coal still holding flame, a long night road's headlights.

Passing the Bucket

Hands palm green bills each Friday morning faculty meeting. You sign and fold them once, twice, maybe four times depending on your tactic. Toss it in the bucket. If your bill gets plucked, you win the pot to cheers and a pat on the back. Ten years I didn't win, but in the hallway outside the NICU, my daughter's breath shallow among the leads and tubes, our Dean of Students hands me an envelope impossibly fat. *More to come,* he says. No platters to return. No thank-you notes. Only this gift in my hands as if they'd passed me the bucket, their names scrawled on each bill.

Making the Call After My Daughter's MRI

Deep breath, nodding at the elevator *dings* descending from the NICU, phone heavy in my pocket, smiling at white coats, scrubs, and strollers, rehearsing *much worse than we thought*. *Ding*—doors open to the lobby. Deep breath and quick strides through croissant and French onion, phone bumping against my keys, kids pointing to fish in their tanks. Through the roar of the revolving door into sun and siren wail. Exhaust and car horns in the drop-off circle. Pulling the phone from my pocket, turning onto Longwood Avenue, past Starbucks and the sandwich shop, walking fast now, dialing Mom's number, and up the steps to the quad of Harvard Medical, facing dogwood trees and Greek columns. In my ear the familiar three-notes, *Hel-lo-o?* and deep breath, deep breath, and I can't speak. A fishing line launches through my silence, through the earpiece; its barbs sink so deep she skips from *Is everything ok?* to *What's wrong, sweetheart?* Constricted throat and words still won't work, but my feet move past pink and white blossoms in sunlight, past the stone steps, and back around the square. Deep breath, a few more steps. Deep breath, a few more steps. Deep breath, and I open my mouth to speak.

New Mercies

I find myself teaching at a school whose mascot is named Wally the Wildcat, and therefore our basketball team has a play called, "Wally," wherein we reverse the ball and the shooting guard receives a weak-side screen, fades to the corner, gets the chance to score.

But it takes me back to the first home game my senior year in the Pit—our high school gym, cut into the small hill on Eighth Avenue. It feels like the whole city is pouring through the doors and filling the u-shaped bleachers. We're wearing our shooting shirts; our best player, Wally, wears Dickies and unlaced boots since low grades keep him from wearing our uniform. When he walks onto the court and throws off his coat to answer a challenge from Big-Head James, its arms float open to hug the gym floor. James checks him the ball and offers a second taunt. Wally jab-steps then glares at him. He crosses left and back to his right, and time stretches out like James's too-late stab at the ball. Wally pushes the ground away and the air crackles beneath his Timberlands. He extends his right hand wide to the side like he is carrying a tray of pizza up to the rim. He climbs the air; we hold our breath. We know that hand is going to smash the ball through the cylinder onto James' head. As he hangs there we look at each other and say, *I will tell my kids about this someday.* Now, I'm hoping they'll live long enough.

His brown arms were slim ropes of muscle, and they carried us to summer league titles. He was entering tenth grade and I was entering twelfth, and we won the Keystone State three-on-three tournament because he was the key all around the key—floating buckets over opponents like they wore shoes of stone. He marked the players who had signed their letters of intent and took them to school early.

On our way to games my little sister looked up at him in awe as he leaned his forehead against our rear window, his gaze searching out the trains roaring on tracks behind the trees. I wonder now what he saw there, looking through glass like he would later during visiting hours.

He worked harder in school the next year, but our principal vowed to keep him off the court in a campaign to *clean up* the school. As if keeping Wally sidelined would sweep the dirt from our systems. The principal didn't want *kids like that* representing our school. So Wally returned to selling on the side. They said he fractured a kid's skull in the school parking lot with the butt of a pistol, but he was gone before the police arrived.

Our kindest community leader shakes his head. *I know you want to help him,* he remarks to our coaches under sad brown eyes, *but there's too much of the street in him.*

That burning summer we play on the legendary Second Avenue courts. Teammates and old heads gather, and the play is fierce. The rubber in our black soles begins to melt on the blacktop. One of the old-timers has a tight fade and a long goatee. The sculpted blades of his shoulders don't hinder the grace of his jump shot, and no one talks trash about his small green shorts. Wally is there, too, and his game still sings. Despite getting mugged and hammered in the lane, his shots land softly on the double rims, falling gently through steel chains.

Looming over us is the Moltrup Steel warehouse. A train wails as if it hasn't stopped hauling cold-finished steel across the waste of brownfield. A girl in a purple tank top sits on a picnic table beside the court. She holds her head between her swaying bracelets as she bobs to the beat of train on tracks. Her purse is on the bench between her feet. Above the glittering splinters of bottles at the edge of the court, the sun gleams on something in her hand. She points towards us. Through tears she screams, *I'm going to fucking kill you, Wally!*

Jai says, *We're out.* Shakes grabs my shoulder and says, *Go, go, go!* And I realize she is aiming a pistol she must have pulled from her purse. The ground bucks beneath our feet as we see the playground scatter. We hop the fence and look back through links of chain to see him: head cocked to one side, arms in the shape of a cross, insisting she *Chill!* Her hand still points at his chest. Between him and her gun stands the old baller with the green shorts. His hands reaching out towards the girl and the gun. Interceding.

Donie says, *What are you looking at, man? Fucking go!* We jam into my car and as we peel away, I look in my mirror to see the old baller speaking peace into the storm. She might be lowering the gun. The sun overhead pulls him into its shadow.

For what new mercies are we spared? A decade later, while my daughter is slowly dying, Wally will allegedly murder a man. Five shots at close range in front of the Elks Club a few blocks from the courts we fled. Though he'll escape to Florida under a fake name, he'll be arrested then extradited. And acquitted. Those courts couldn't hold him, either. Four years after, at the same spot outside the Elks Club, he'll be shot and the friend with him will be killed. He'll swear vengeance on the cat who ran at them from the darkness beyond Dollar General and opened fire—another player we used to ball with. Another change of possession.

I still see Wally poised at the rim like so many of our dreams. Where his coat struck the floor, the outline of an angel remains in the dust. He cocks the ball back, triumphant, and flushes the ball through that great orange circle. The ball bounces away, and the backboard is still shaking as explosions of *oh!* and *damn!* are lost in the hum of the bleachers.

As Lawrence Timmons Tackles Derek Mason, I Think of Home

For Carl and Lisa

The game's tied when Flacco drops back in the pocket
and lofts the ball over the blitz, over our
collective groan. Another win streak about to end

as Mason catches and turns upfield, the sleek
raven on his helmet squawking, *Nevermore!*
I'm not thinking of Steeler Santas

shaking fists a few rows ahead, nor the bridges
we've crossed to be here. I'm not thinking
of the Ohio, the Allegheny, the Monongahela—

rivers whose name this field once wore. Instead
I wonder how this crowd might thunder
in my daughter's weak chest, or how many blankets

her nurses snugged on her this warm December day
back in Boston. Before the groans exit
our mouths we see a gold and black streak.

It happens that fast. Timmons closing in
at an angle exactly wrong and exactly right
to baptize Mason into two layers of sound.

I know I shouldn't praise this violence. A bit
is in the water of this town where I was raised,
where my friends have brought me

to knock a bit of wanting from my chest,
and we all can see Mason's a northbound train
on a southbound track. When the hit arrives

his purple cleats lift from the turf and the *crack*
tolls through the stadium like a rung bell.
I feel it in my teeth, as if it's my fillings

that have been loosened by the hit that's decleated
my family. My son's lying in the grass
where his plastic truck rammed the curb. Soon

he'll stagger to his feet, fine, but clutching his neck
as if his opponent got it worse and will not rise
from the settling dust. My wife's back is to him

while she scoots our daughter's wheelchair
from the shade. Our daughter whose brain's been
pummeled more than Iron Mike Webster's will not

struggle to her feet, will not walk away from this.

Night Nurses

Though other night nurses sit at our dining room table to enter notes or rest until the next stat check, Kadeeja sits in our flower-embroidered rocker, which she pulls to our daughter's bedside beside the oxygen concentrator. She watches over our son as well since he shares the room. She likes to pull back the curtain of the closest window to let the moon in. Says it is all the light she needs. When we ask her to switch to a Wednesday night, she agrees. My wife and I use the Tuesday hours for a daytime nurse to stay with our daughter while a close friend watches our son. We head to Hale Street for Tuesday night's half-price burgers. At home, we finish our daughter's respiratory therapies, administer the last of her meds, thank our nurse and babysitter and tuck in our children. Alone at last we fall into bed for a few minutes finding hilarious glorious comfort in each other's breath and body and the darkness doesn't seem so thick. We stumble out of our bedroom, naked in the moonlit hallway, and make our way to the bathroom, pausing at the door of our daughter's room to peek at our sleeping kids. This is when we lock eyes with Kadeeja. She's sitting in her usual rocker by our daughter's bedside, her long fingers covering her dropped jaw. Before we can wonder if it's her mistake or ours, before we can wonder how she made her way into the building or whether it really matters anyway, the three of us are frozen like that. She with her hand blanketing her mouth, my wife and I with our hands across our bodies. And maybe that's the nurses' role. Coming into our home to find us raw and unguarded. Trying to help us through the long night.

She Kept a Strange Vigil in the Hall That Night

After Marie Howe and Walt Whitman

Praise to my department head who raced across
campus, five-foot frame growing as she strode

inside the dorm to plant her feet outside
our door, one arm raised as if to say

You shall not pass to teachers and to
headmasters, to students and to duty staff.

Praise her, whose glare wilted boys throwing
a football down the hall, who turned aside kids

needing passes signed, who only unbarred the way
for family or medical staff. When the hall quieted,

her knitting needles gleamed, twisting stitches
in their course. She tucked soft yarn into rows,

one line neat above the other. Praise her who
in the light of a desk lamp opened her book

to a paperclipped page and underlined a passage.
She didn't hear our daughter's rapid breathing

or our nurse saying, *Soon now.* Not until a ghostly
silence settled did she depart her post for home.

I don't know if she knows she knitted an invisible
coat that fell around our shoulders as we folded

our daughter's blanket, tucking it carefully
under her feet, our child with kisses never again

on earth responding. We rose and carried her down
the hallway cleared for us, out into the slowing rain,

halting behind the hearse, lingering in the night
as clouds scattered and new stars steeled upwards.

In the Circle

We wheel our daughter beside the orbs and butterflies strung from tall windows to help the light sashay in. We prop her between us on the preschool carpet, her classmates velcroed in standers or reclining in foam chairs with their orthopedic vests. We sing and drum each child's name, ask our friend: *Is your son back to eating by mouth?* The music therapist's beads clack a beat as she strums, "If You're Happy and You Know It." We replace the words *your face will surely* with *you really want to.* Beside the ache near our lungs is something like joy.

In the circle we help our kids to clap. Watch them shimmer. Half will die in a couple years. At each funeral we'll embrace like college friends at weddings. I take my daughter's large hands—*mitts*, my buddy calls them with a nod—and we clap against disaster.

In Praise of Dependence

Because *Don't Weaken* ripples across a powerlifter's shirt just below the bar he's pressing off his chest. Because *Don't weaken* seems stacked between concrete blocks in the Assistant Dean's office wall. Because above his head the signed Tom Brady, perfect in its frame, seems to say, *Don't weaken.* It's the same story: checklists unchecked, emails unanswered, reports unwritten. Every absence, every meeting, every request builds my resistance to asking for aid. I'd rather feel guilty than helpless. But he's already made a schedule of ways he'll lighten my workload. As I mumble the latest of my daughter's bad news, a new baseline, another ICU stint, I look up at the lens focusing his sight. It's tears.

Through the Attic Window

My wife and I are crawling on the pavement in the twilight outside a McDonald's rest stop, looking for the oil cap that slipped from my fingers and fell into the engine of our Honda Odyssey. We had the van serviced before we left, but the oil light blinked on a few miles ago. In the back of the van, behind my two-month-old son and two-and-a-half-year-old daughter, are my daughter's fifty-pound oxygen concentrator, her air compressor, cough assist machine, nebulizer, two space heaters, bottle warmer, power cords, tubing for the machines, an IV pole and base, and two 680-liter oxygen tanks. It's almost Thanksgiving and we're making the twelve-hour drive from Northeast Massachusetts to Western Pennsylvania to reunite with my parents, relatives, and friends as close as family. With our daughter's health, we don't know if we'll have another chance. We haven't even made it out of the state.

Before we left, I started the van and cranked the heat so it would be warm when I brought our daughter out. My wife clipped our two-month-old son into his car seat while I returned to the apartment. On the lap of one of her nurses, our daughter waited until I slid my right hand under her legs and my left hand across her shoulder blades, then carried her out into the cold.

*

After my daughter was moved to the ICU for another aspiration pneumonia, the pediatric palliative care team began meeting with us. They said, "Tell us about what's most important to you." They said, "Tell us about a good day for your daughter." They said, "Tell us about a hard day."

*

My wife calls her dad who says the oil cap will probably fall out during the drive. He tells us to stop at an Autozone and get a replacement cap when we arrive in Western Pennsylvania. We do.

*

My wife and I avoid playgrounds and toddlers our daughter's age. Maybe it doesn't kill me to sit next to Cora at our weekly residential life meetings because I love her parents. As we discuss students, she's on her mom's lap, reaching for the water bottle on the conference table. She leans forward, one hand on the table. She hooks a finger into a carabiner on the bottle's handle and pulls it over. The miracle of it. She reaches. She takes it. She drinks.

*

In the back of the van are a box of allergen-free nutritional supplements, a box of electrolytes, a box of large disposable pads and a box of diapers, a box of Zevex bags with piping to fit her feeding pump, a box of Farell valves that connect to the pump and release the pressure in her belly, a box of G-tube ports, a bag of eight-inch attachments that connect to the valve in her belly, bags of oral syringes of every size, a bag of oxygen and nebulizer and cough assist masks, a bag of adapters and replacement filters for each machine, a bag of suction catheters, a bag of pediatric enemas.

*

At a professional development presentation on executive functions, I looked up at a slide with pictures of the brain projected large above me. Each lobe was lit in different colors above the cerebellum. My mind titled the slide with the words "global brain injury."

*

In the rear view mirror, my daughter's ponytails brush the collar of her paisley-flowered vest. As she brings her head forward, her breathing relaxes. I reach back to brush my fingers against her cold cheek. Once, in the ICU, her temperature dropped to ninety degrees after her bath because I wasn't more vigilant at warning the nurses of her hypothermia.

I start to pass an old Civic with its flashers on when a truck roars by. I jerk back into our lane. No highway tower lights. No headlights across the divider. My daughter's feeding pump beeps from the back seat. My wife turns it off and clamps the feeding tube. The click echoes in the quiet.

In Pennsylvania, the kerosene heater my parents bought for our visit blasts heat into whichever room our daughter's sitting. At a reunion with family friends, my best friend's mom bounces her gently up and down on the couch and cackles with delight. Our daughter beholds her wide-eyed, and everyone laughs. When it's time to go, we shake hands and hug around the circle. Some of them we will never see again. None of them will see her again.

On a snowy Thanksgiving we drive up to my uncle's house for a big family gathering. As we walk into the large kitchen my dad stands tall and raises his hands for attention. He tells everyone that we're glad to be there, but that my wife and I don't have the capacity today to talk about our daughter and the updates regarding her condition. The relief that pours over us gives us the energy to float through the day. In the living room, beside a fireplace churning out its heat, my Grandma holds our daughter's hand for the last time. Our healthy son is passed between aunts and cousins like the football on television.

The next day it's time to pack up. My mom and sister can't help showering our kids with new outfits. My dad bought our son another tiny Steeler hoodie. We cram them in the back with the rest, and with tearful goodbyes we drive towards home.

*

Sometimes the obvious clangs on my head like a cartoon anvil. I've always had trouble articulating my daughter's struggles and joys. I listen to two disability scholars discuss how difficult it is to find language for parenting outside the self-help, future-directed, most-possible river of advice. *Clang.* It's hard to explain because it's hard to explain.

*

I turn the heat up a few degrees, settle deeper into my seat and stare at the white dotted lines of the New York Thruway. My wife's voice rises from the backseat darkness: "It's freezing in here."

I can't keep the rolling eyes out of my voice: "It's 76. I'll turn it up to 78."

A few miles later: "Are you sure the heat's on? Her cheeks are freezing."

In the rear view, our daughter's pink hat pokes out above the sparkling Mylar blankets my wife is positioning around her.

We passed an exit five minutes ago. No new signs. I fiddle with the dials hoping the heat will magically start working. I turn it off and turn it back on. Nothing.

*

In the back of the van are boxes of Pulmicort and Atrovent vials, Albuterol ampules, the Lupron Depot injection, Klonopin, Methadone, Phenobarbital, Zantac, Keppra, Senna, Calcium, Calciferol. In the freezer bag: ampules of Tobramycin,

Ceftin and Neurontin. Pantoprazole and Topomax mixed at a compounding pharmacy in Ipswich. Ziplocs of MiraLAX, Melatonin, and Fluticasone, of Maalox, Mylicon, Tylenol, Motrin, and multivitamins, of surgical lubricant and pink oral swabs. A Ziploc with pill crusher, mortar, and pestle.

*

At my gym we run a mile with a twenty-pound medicine ball. I try shifting the weight to my hip, my shoulder, my head. A runner passing me says, "No easy way to carry it."

*

In the back of the van are a bottle of Scope to keep the suction container from smelling awful, her Bumble Ball and pink Slinky, a light-up toy fish tank, the light wave machine from Perkins School for the Blind, Stomahesive for treating her g-tube site, a bag of peroxide, bacitracin, long cotton swabs, a bag of thermometers, lotions, ointments, a bag with Ankle-Foot Orthotics, a hard plastic body jacket, a bag of books and DVDs with strong female protagonists.

*

I look at our thermostat. The needle's beyond the H. I take a deep breath and wait for the thermostat to return to normal. It doesn't. Still no exit signs. Cold rain smacks the windshield. The van starts to jerk and shake. "Come on," I tell the engine. Needle still jammed in the red. The shaking grows stronger.

When an engine overheats, the aluminum material begins to warp and swell. The cylinder walls and pistons start to bend and crack. Oil is forced past the piston rings and into the engine, where it burns.

I keep my breathing calm but clutch the wheel with two fists as if my grip might shove us further forward. "Come on," I say again. No other headlights on either side of the road.

When an engine overheats, the pistons scrape against the cylinder walls, knocking and grinding as the engine begins to lose pressure until the warped pistons break and the engine seizes up completely.

We round a bend into a long climb. "Come on." I'm yelling now. We jerk and shake up the hill as I clench the wheel. I see an exit sign. "Come on. Please." I hear a banging sound beneath the hood and we begin to slow. We're getting closer. "Come on. Come on." We drift onto the off-ramp as the power steering fails. The engine sounds like all machinery that clamors for help it isn't getting.

*

We no longer enter the hospital through the ER. When our daughter's sick, we call our case worker who reserves a room on the ninth floor. Like it's the Hilton.

*

In the back of the van is my daughter's Kid Kart wheelchair, and piled around it are the jeans, sweats, shirts, and fleeces my wife and I have shoved into bags. Our son's pack 'n play, bouncy seat, clothes, toys, and the Baby Bjorn baby carrier are stuffed into the remaining spaces like leftovers in a fridge. We didn't have room for his stroller.

*

Casting its light across the highway ramp where I'm standing and waiting to cross, a rodent's face grins atop a Wonder Woman body. Her star-spangled arm clutches a gas nozzle. Betty Beaver's Fuel Stop. I hunch against the frigid drizzle. Behind me, our minivan rests quiet on the shoulder. As I step into the road, I wonder if this cold will kill my daughter.

The guy from AAA says there are a bunch of hotels within 10 miles and gives me the number of the Hilton. Nicer than we've ever stayed, but we'll use the credit card. Maybe we can stay in comfort and get a refrigerator for our daughter's medications.

"A tow truck can be there in an hour," he says.

Betty Beaver's parking lot is Ford and Chevy. Mud flaps and gun racks. Inside, my quarter-zip and sweats make me the only one without a hunting vest and flannel. The young woman behind the counter is chatting with one of the hunters, John Deere hats pulled low over their eyes. She looks up as I approach.

*

Once, driving through the mountains near Lock Haven, two

eighteen-wheelers slowing both lanes ahead, I watched a hawk leap from its branch on the embankment. It winged directly into the machines barreling down. I flinched for the trucks' swerve or brakes when in some trick of physics the great bird wheeled back above the windshield and over the smokestacks into the blue sky.

*

At Betty Beaver's counter, the young woman with the trucker hat is glaring at me. I tell her, "My daughter has a complicated medical condition, and our car just broke down on the off ramp. Our heat isn't working, so can I bring her in here if I need to?"

A pause, then: "Of course, hon. That's why we're here."

*

What appear to be a tow truck's flashing lights unblur to reveal a police cruiser instead. I tell the officer about our minivan and explain the need to get our daughter somewhere warm. Then I ask if he knows where the Hilton is.

He looks down at me, "We have one hotel here. It's no Hilton. But I'll give them a call and bring you over."

My wife grabs my shoulder. "Sir," I blurt, "we can't leave our van. It's full of medical equipment our daughter needs tonight."

He considers. "You think your van can make it another two miles?"

"I don't," I say. "But we can try." I turn the ignition and

there's a fluttering whine. I pump the gas and the van sputters and shakes to life. We hustle into our seats before we stall, and we wheeze back onto the ramp, turning right and following the officer down past the dark windows of old factories pressing close to the road. As I ease on the gas, we buck forward like I'm stomping the pedals. My wife sits between our kids, clutching a hand to each of their chests. I coast through intersections, scared to stop. We shudder across a bridge and along the river. Without warning the officer turns off the main road and up a hill. I swerve to follow him as the oil and engine lights flash on the dashboard.

"Where the heck is he going?" I ask.

In answer my wife points through the windshield.

The motel sits there on the hill. Our minivan coughs to a stop beside a rusted maroon Tacoma that's the lone vehicle in the lot.

*

When our daughter was almost two, our social worker helped us apply for the Catastrophic Illness in Children Relief Fund. We combined all the funding we received with all we had in savings to buy this used Honda Odyssey for her and her equipment.

*

The officer asks us if there's anything else he can do. My wife and I look at each other and shrug. A Victorian house looms behind the motel. In every horror plot, this is the beginning of the end. A family seeks shelter in the rain. The caretaker waits behind the desk. With his thin hair combed back from the bald and down to his shoulders, he looks like a cryptkeeper with blue jeans and glasses. We stand there, my son cozy against me beneath my jacket. Our daughter is covered in blankets, my wife massaging her chest and shoulders to warm her up.

"Andy," he says, introducing himself and extending his hand.

Andy shows us the room. Mildew climbs up the air conditioner, spreads into the wall and ceiling. Large stains and clumps of ragged lint line the carpet. He seems sorry about the mess. We forget to ask about a refrigerator.

*

Once, in the dorm kitchen, my student lifted a water bottle from the dishwasher to the cabinet shelf where it fell back to the counter, straight into a juice glass. As it shattered, he punched the cabinet door, screaming, "Why?" He stepped into the hallway, kicked a closet door and said, "Of all places, why did it have to be right there?"

*

We find a fridge underneath the bathroom counter. We crank the heat. I race back and forth across the lot to grab the space heaters and bags of meds. Our daughter seems stable, though I wonder who will come if I dial 911, and where they might take her.

We get to work wiping surfaces, setting up the room, unpacking each item from the van. And so the night passes. One item, one task at a time. We carefully construct a nest for each kid and lay them gently down. By the time we climb in bed beside them, we don't question how clean the sheets might be.

*

After the morning meds and feedings, we step out the door into a day that feels more like May than late November. Andy tells us of a deli a mile down the road. We buckle our daughter into her Kid Kart and bundle her in blankets, then snug our son into the baby carrier and walk to buy breakfast, groceries, cleaning supplies. When we cross the bridge in daylight, a bronze plaque tells us the town founder has my last name. My wife snaps a photo of me and the kids in front of the name of some perhaps long-lost ancestor.

The deli staff lets us borrow a grocery cart and we wheel it the mile back to the motel in the morning sun. Andy advises us on car shops and looks at the engine while I make calls to get my classes and dorm duties covered.

*

Once, in class, my students and I studied Buster Keaton's choreography. He rubs a crick in his neck. Behind him, the entire side of a house tears loose from its frame. It plunges toward his back and crashes down, but the open attic window falls around him. He whirls around with those great bewildered eyes, standing unharmed in the one perfect spot amid the wreckage, surveying the damage that missed him. The props and plans of the gag perfected.

*

The mechanic tells us the oil cap fell into the radiator where the fan chopped it to pieces and drove a shard into the coolant reservoir, which leaked until it emptied. I feel again the oil cap slipping from my fingers.

*

My wife's dad hitches a trailer to his Chevy and drives from a state away, then crosses into another to pick up the van, saving us a thousand dollars in towing fees. He'll tow it hundreds of miles further to a dealership in Massachusetts with the best price on a used Odyssey engine, saving us thousands more. We'll get the van back after New Year's.

*

Once, as we're driving down an interstate, we pass one of those weigh stations with its lights flashing. I imagine an official waving us over to a giant scale. We take my daughter's supplies and equipment out of the van and place them one by one on the weight sensors. The total keeps growing. Five hundred pounds. Six. And I'm thinking how one day soon she will be free of all of it.

*

My buddy arrives from two states away in his parents' minivan. It's an Odyssey the same year as ours. Instead of dark gray, it's champagne colored. As if we're swapping ash for celebration. Together, he and I pack the van again. In the front passenger seat I toss the venison jerky and gummy bears I bought from the deli. A bag of chips and bottles of water. A John Deere hat I bought as a souvenir. In my pocket are the notes Andy helped me write for my next conversation with the dealership.

I ease my daughter into her car seat. I clip her in and tuck her pink and white blanket around her. Then I attach her little pillow with the rainbow stars to the Velcro strips on her shoulder straps. She leans her left cheek against it and peers over my shoulder at the sun breaking through the clouds. I kiss her on the eyebrow and arrange two more blankets on her lap. My wife clunks my son's seat into its base and slides herself into the seat between our kids. I hop back into shotgun, my buddy at the wheel, and we pull away.

Charlotte's Blankets

They descend like a pink curtain over my wife when her students hear we're having a girl. There's the pale yellow one her mom knit. There's the one with green ridges. The peach one soft like her skin. The one checkered pink. The one robin's egg blue, best for swaddling our daughter tight.

There's the one my mom made, yellow and blue knots like bows on a present. Another her mom knit, lavender collared with white. There's the quilt the NICU gave us, sprinkled with drops of her blood.

They descend like a dream, each lavender and yellow square holding a hundred fluttering flowers. The one with blue and brown polka dots. The one pale green trying always to slither off the bed during hospital stays. The salmon one huddling my wife and daughter for a nap.

We stack them one on the other, trying to keep her warm. The orange one. The one folded over her like a red heart. The one with brown flannel draped on top like holy exhaustion. The navy blue electric one from her palliative care team. The one with stars and astronauts. The one rippling mountains of white, pink, and gold. The one rainbowed on gray wool. Like glittering static prismed across hospital sheets. Like oil in a puddle catching light.

They descend like talismans. The one with kaleidoscopic pastels mailed from Michigan. The one stitched by the St. Boniface Quilters in Sea Cliff. The one woven by artists in Malawi with Noah and the animals exiting the ark underneath a rainbow. The ones lavishing a white and pink tower over her right side while she nestles between a plush dolphin and a clownfish, as if together they might swim her out our window and across the moonlit ocean below.

G-Tube Ode

When all attempts to deliver
by mouth what our daughter needs
will choke and kill her
you are the door
cut through ab and stomach lining
a silicone frame some make
into a sign for vegetative states
you who we resisted
of whom they say *common*
for kids with her type
of difficulties
you a reminder
of the wonder of avocados
squelched from cheek pocket
to cheek pocket
you coil on her belly
a twin-mouthed serpent
sunning itself
when we forget to click your clamp
before opening the end
of your tube then all the food
and meds we've prepared for her
pour back into our laps

when the pressure mounts
no outlet for her gas expanding
until we attach the big syringe
holding it upright
so the bubbles climb
towards heaven
you the site
of bolus and infusion
which the funeral director told us
he pulled from her body
as he prepared it
his voice trembling
the site now open
like the hole in the earth
to receive her
the only blemish
in the smooth lake of her skin
scratching his head
he confessed he wept
he who has laid so many children to rest
wanting her to enter the grave whole
without your silicone shell
that does not know pain
does not know decay
that will not rejoin the earth

Through the Concourse Din

Across the tall counter a machine-gun thunk of keys. The agent's eyes scan our car seats, our son Will's stroller, our daughter Charlotte rolling her shoulders in her adaptive wheelchair, her oxygen stowed beneath. That's why we're here: only Delta allows oxygen tanks on board.

The agent shakes her head, "Usually they call us. Why didn't you call?" A staccato click of keys. We glance back at Katie, the Make-a-Wish aide rocking our son's stroller too fast. Sarah, my brother's wife turned part-time nurse, shows her the proper motion.

"The arrangements are easy," Katie said two months prior as our coffee mugs steamed beside strewn forms, "we do trips like this all the time." She and another volunteer talked us through the process from our living room couch, pointing where to sign. "I love Florida," she said, "it'll be such a nice break for you and your family."

The ticketing line snakes behind us. Luggage shifts and creaks. The agent shakes her head again: "Pre-board for special needs is about to start. There's no way you can make it." Sarah lets go of Charlotte's hand and switches on the machine to suction her mouth. Some in the crowd stare, some pretend not to look.

"We're with Make-a-Wish" says my wife, Meryl, her fin-

gers tented at each eyebrow as if these words might conjure help. "Isn't there anything you can do? How could they not tell us a detail like this?" She looks back at Katie, who is watching the queue at a new line Delta has opened.

The agent slaps tags on our bags. Sighs. "I'll call ahead," she offers, "but they won't delay a flight for you." I look from her to Meryl, my hands and voice shaking into my only words: "We have to try." We step away from the counter, face the terminal, begin to walk.

In the skylights' cold glint, travelers spill around our son's stroller. Sarah takes it from Katie, quickens her strides. From the way my wife's hand bulges inside her purse, I know she's gripping her bottle of Ativan. She pulls out her hand and shoves the diaper bag higher up her shoulder while wheeling Charlotte forward. She brushes her fingers against the flat escalator rail like it's a river rushing past. I lug the backpack and med bag and car seat already heavy in my arms. We glance back and note Katie lagging a court's length behind. Her blue high heels clack in the concourse din.

When we began to consider the trip seriously, we joined our daughter's palliative care doctor and social worker at a table in the hospital library to think through the question, "What do you envision for your family?" This was something they frequently asked, gently sharing ways we might live with our terminally ill three-year-old. They suggested we write a list of pros and cons:

Pro: Humid heat so right we can take Charlotte for

walks without the five blankets her hypothermia usually requires.

Pro: Give Kids the World has its own rides and playgrounds built for all styles of wheelchairs.

Pro: Warm wading pools on each block of the special needs village.

Con: she could die.

We planned test outings to Boston and Rockport, prepped meds in diners, practiced rinsing her feeding pump in public bathrooms. We took notes in our journals about where the challenges might catch us.

When Katie trips, she holds her arms like a plane and tilts toward the wall, ankles wobbling as she stumbles to the floor. Relief and shame fight in the red blotching her cheeks. Meryl helps her check for a sprain. Sarah uses the moment to adjust Will's stroller seat and slow his squirming. Charlotte stirs under her blankets and raises an eyebrow as if she's amused by it all.

In the pause my thoughts become knives: *Here we are, arrangements made, and we can't even make it to the plane. We're not the people to take trips like this. Charlotte can't handle it. Who were we kidding?* Then a jolt in my gut as I think of our parents and siblings and their families who bought tickets to fly down and meet us.

Meryl helps Katie struggle to her feet. With tears in her eyes she bids us good luck. We lurch forward, a little slower than before, and pass another flat escalator. Amid the throng gliding towards us, a woman in Pepto-Bismol pink and an ID badge is passing slower travelers. She's backlit by sun through the skylights, but as she floats closer, she seems to look right at us. Something about her manner cues the eighties jingle in my brain: *Del-ta! We love to fly and it shows!* She steps off the moving walkway into a new shaft of light and holds out her hand. Says, "I'm Debbie."

In awe my wife whispers, "Debbie Delta?"

Debbie grins. "That's right." And now we're all laughing. "We don't have a lot of time, so let's get you to your flight," she says and whisks us onward at a half-jog, rose perfume in her wake. We find our strides matching hers; the bags and car seat I carry feel lighter. When we reach the line for security, she unhooks the belt between stanchions and we veer to the new lane she's made.

She beckons us toward officers who wave wands over us and across our daughter's Kid Kart, at which I clench my fists. But Sarah is scooping Will from his stroller so I take a deep breath, fold it, and place it on the conveyor beside the car seat.

When we retrieve our gear, we follow the clacks of Debbie's strides towards the distant right wall. It looks like we're approaching a service door you'd see in a highway tunnel. As we get closer, we realize it's an elevator.

Charlotte makes a shrieking gasp over the din that halts us mid-stride. Meryl drops to her knees to give her chest PT: rhythmic whacks with a cupped hand. She pushes down on her chest with a firm, gentle, massage. I turn to Debbie and tell her, "She does this. It's okay. We'll let you know if it's not." After a few more thumps to Charlotte's chest, I suction fluid from her mouth. Meryl offers her a pink oral swab that she licks and begins to chew contentedly. We step into the elevator.

"It's going to be hard either way," our most direct doctor told us, "so make the decision that best addresses the quality of experience for your family." When Meryl and I glanced at each other, she continued, "You have your list, and you've planned for months. Trust your gut."

Under *Pros*, we wrote, *Our family all together. A place equipped for her needs. A last trip with all of us.*

Under *Cons* we underlined, *She could die.*

The elevator doors open on a deserted concourse as if we've traveled to an alternate dimension. Debbie steps into the emptiness and calls back, "Bathroom? No better chance." She unclips her phone from her belt and starts barking orders. It's so quiet I join Meryl to wheel our kids to the women's bathroom for quick diaper changes.

In our living room, Katie told us, "We're so glad we can make your wish come true," like she was reciting a script. Meryl and I smiled and thanked her but shared a look we both understood to mean we were thinking of time travel or a parallel universe where Charlotte didn't suffer a global brain injury during her birth. True wishes.

A last dash brings us to our gate. The waiting area's empty and the plane's already boarded. Debbie's pink jacket is huddled with the gate attendants until she turns, twirling her badge round one finger, and waves us over. Smiles. Walks us down the gangway tube where baggage handlers take the Kid Kart and stroller.

Debbie blows kisses and waves and then she's a flash of pink heading back up the ramp. The flight attendant helps us enter the plane and take the first-class seats Debbie switched us into. This surprise won't stop Meryl's panic—she'll need two Ativan to get through the flight, and I'll need more in the crowds at Magic Kingdom, whisked to the front of lines for attractions Charlotte's too sick to ride.

At Give Kids the World, the supplies and machines we've had shipped from the tri-state area won't be there when we arrive. But we'll wheel her across the village, the sun pouring its heat on us in a blessing of sweat. We won't be able to stop touching her cheek, feeling its strange new warmth.

We'll wheel her into a chapel whose stone walls and columns and vaulted arches gleam with stars. On each is written a sick child's name. As they laser Charlotte's name into a star and hoist it to the small sky beside the others, we'll look up in perfect silence. We'll imagine the stories that brought them here. Or didn't. We'll wonder what might be possible if they had someone like Debbie, but with the power to fix things. Someone to arrange the pieces and part the lines and help the real wish take flight.

Acknowledgements

Thank you to the journals who accepted the following pieces for publication:

"In the Circle" and "G-Tube Ode"—*The Adroit Journal*
"Night Nurses"—*Tampa Review*

Thank you to the medical staff who gave such wonderful care to our daughter Charlotte and to us and who do the same for so many other children and families who need their exquisite skill and dedication, especially Cape Ann Early Intervention, PediPathways, and the Coordinated Care Service and Pediatric Advanced Care Team at Children's Hospital Boston. Overwhelming gratitude as well to Charlotte's home nurses and to the staff, volunteers, and incredible parents who form the community of The Perkins School for the Blind Infant-Toddler program.

Thank you to our incredible friends at Landmark School for your love and support, and thank you to the extraordinary students and faculty at The Ethel Walker School.

Thank you to Lisa Fay Coutley and Diane Goettel for your wonderful work at Black Lawrence Press, for believing in this book, and for bringing it out into the world.

For their poems, mentorship, and the inspiration of their work, I want to thank Brad Davis, Erin Broudo, Erin Ott, Henk Rossouw, John Murillo, Nicole Sealey, Craig Morgan Teicher, Tina Chang, Edgar Kunz, and Naomi Shihab Nye. A big thank you to Matt Blazer for his friendship and partnership in writing pursuits, and for introducing me to the Parker Jotter. And thank you to Dave Thacker for the vigilant, illuminating, and encouraging reading that helped shape this manuscript.

Thank you to all of my family for your support, but especially Andrew and Sarah Frey, Kim Frey, Michael and Erin Cartona, Nicole, Andrew, and Maddie Ellrod, and Nick and Coreen Faraco. Thank you as well to Brad and Sue Frey, my first teachers and readers. Will, Ben, and Josie, thank you for inspiring me and helping me make this *cozy mess*. And Meryl, love, thanks for each *brief hour and week*.

Jenessa Lu

SCOTT FREY is a poet and educator who grew up in Western Pennsylvania and teaches English at Pine Meadow Academy in Windsor Locks, Connecticut. He and his wife, Meryl, run a non-profit charity, The Charlotte Frey Foundation, whose mission is to help children with multiple handicaps and life-threatening illnesses and their families improve their quality of life. His book, *Heavy Metal Nursing*, won the Tampa Review Prize for poetry. Among other places, his work has been published or is forthcoming in *Passages North*, *december magazine*, *The Adroit Journal*, *Bellevue Literary Review*, *New York Quarterly*, and *The Missouri Review*, where he was awarded the Perkoff Prize for poetry. He and his family live in Granby, Connecticut.

.